Rooted In Love
(A Selection Of Poems)
by Dante LeGare

Rooted In Love (A Selection Of Poems)

By Dante L. LeGare

Contents

A Prayer 6

Fear Not 7

Do It All 8

Beloved 9

Prisoner Freed 10

Monkey See, Monkey Do 13

Keep It Together 14

Cold Turkey 18

Live 19

Divine Multiplication 21

Jesus Christ 22

The Dream 23

My Enemy 25

God Is the Reason (Why I Love You) 26

You Are Not Alone (Divine Multiplication II) 27

Guardian Angels 29

Devine Subtraction 31

True Love 35

The Boy 36

Queen In Her Own Right 38

Real Work, True Worth 39

HEART/MIND 39

To Thine Own Self Be True 40

Hidden Away 42

Rooted 44

The Close 45

Acknowledgements 46

Dedication

This book is dedicated,

I say, dedicated to,

I say, to the most beautiful,

I say, most Lovely,

I say, most giving woman

In the world.

She who understands me

And still chooses to

Love me, and stay

In my life;

Keeping her vows,

Those she took as my wife.

I love you and the Spirit God put in you.

A Prayer

Forgive me my heart

For, I am a wretched man.

Thank God for His saving grace

For, that is the only way I can stand.

F̲E̲A̲R̲ ̲N̲O̲T̲

There was a time

Long ago

I had cried because of fear.

There was a time

Long ago

I had trembled because the devil was near

But now

I don't

Feel the same.

I don't even

Capitalize

The devil's name.

Oh! My Lord

Told me

"Fear not…!"

As He told

Those before me

"Fear not…"

Do It All

A songbird sings

A fish swims

An eagle soars

A lion roars

A rooster crows

But what does a man do?

A man does it all!

BELOVED

Beloved, are you there?

My voice can you hear?

My love can you feel?

Do you know that it's real?

Beloved, do not fear.

Be courageous I am near.

Have faith in Me, My child.

You'll be with Me in a short while.

But for now let Me guide your steps.

Let Me show you the way.

Walk in My footprints in the sand.

In the sand they lay.

Seek Me always.

Walk and pray.

PRISONER FREED

I want, I want, I want!
    All I keep hearing
        Is I want!
And what is it
    My voice is blaring
        That I want?!

This and that
    And those over there
        I'm tired of it
"I WANT!"
    Is all I hear.

And it's my voice.
    The desires of my heart,
        The greed of my mind,
The lust of my flesh,
    My spiritual bind.
        My shackles,
My chains,
    My confines,
        Restraints!

    'Do you want to be free?
    Do you want to get away?
        Fall on your knees,
        My son, and pray.'

Who said that?
    Who's there?
        I can't see you.
            I'm blind.
I'm surprised
    I hear
        Past the screams
            Of my mind.

I feel comfort
    And peace
        In the presence
            Of you
Say again
    To me
        What it is
    I must do!

    'Listen, my son,
        For again I say
        Fall on your knees,
        Bow your head, and pray.'

Who are you
    Who speaks
        And causes me to tremble
            With fear
And makes me
    Feel peace
        With every word that
        I hear

Your presence is
    So great
        It seems to fill this
            Whole room.
Where are my
    Enemies?
        Did you seal
            Their doom?

    'I Am The Lord Almighty.
    Pray to me and see;
    Call on the Lord
    I will set you free.'

What am I
    To you
        That you will do as
            You have said?
No more than
    A thief
        That lie, cheat, and steal to
            Get ahead.
My Lord, how
    Can You
        Forgive me the wrong
            I've done?
D'You know the guilt
    I bear?
        D'You know all

                    I've done?

I did not know you as a
        Young man
                I do not know
                        You now
And you expect me to call
        On You
                And to kneel,
                        And bow?
Him I do
        Not know
                Is him I
                        Do not trust;
And you say
        Bowing
                To you is
                        A must?

        'So you want to stay in
        The situation you're in?
        Then we will talk no more.
        This conversation will end.'

No, my Lord,
        Don't leave…

            'Wait, wait, wait, wait
            Who said I was
                Your Lord?

            You denied Me.
            Your words, your tongue,
                Your sword.'

But, Lord, I don't
        Know you.
                Teach me
                        Your way.
Teach me who
        You are.
                Teach me
                        Today.

Show me mercy,
        O Lord,
                I'm dying day
                        By day.

                Remove my shackles,
                    O Lord,
                        I kneel, I bow,
                                I pray.
                Lord, I've heard
                    Of you –
                        Some good,
                                Some bad –
                I've never
                    Met you
                        And cared not if
                                I had.
                But now you
                    Are here
                        With me in
                                This cell.
                Free me
                    I pray
                        Lead me
                                From hell.
                Lord, are
                    You there?
                        You have not
                                Left me?
                I will call on
                    You, Lord,
                        Until You
                                Bless me.

                Speak to me, Lord,
                    I pray.
                        Speak to me, Lord,
                                I say.
                Don't leave me ,
                    But teach me,
                        Teach me, Lord,
                                Your way.

                    'I am here and will do
                    That which I have said.
                    I will loose your shackles
                    And feed you my bread.

                    I will teach you My way.
                    I'll show you mercy.
                    I will free your spirit,

And keep you near Me.

For I see you are humbled,
Bowed head, bended knee;
I hear your prayer,
Your cry unto Me.

I'll teach you my love
And righteousness.
I'll teach you justice,
And faithfulness.

But I need to know,
For you shall slip and fall;
Would you get up and fight,
Or stay where you fall?'

My Lord, I
   Believe
      You already know what
         I'd do
If you stay
   With me
      I would stay
         With You.
I would get up
   And fight
      So long as you are
         By my side
For you will be all things
   To me
      Including that place
         Where I hide

'Then know that I will
Never leave you nor forsake you.
You are free right now
I have removed your shackles.

Open your eyes, son,
See my glory, my splendor;
See my joy in you.
Since to me you surrendered.

I am the Lord, your God,
Your Father, your Creator;
You are My son, My servant
I will show you great favor.

Most of all I will show you
Love, truth, joy, and peace.
You will help spread the gospel
Tell the world about me.

And in the day,
In due time,
When all is said and done
You'll sit in heaven
By my side
With your brothers
and sisters,
My son.'

Thank You,
Lord

Monkey See, Monkey Do

I once had a monkey, whose name was Pat. He could steal hearts at the drop of a hat. I took him everywhere, no matter where I went. He was like my little boy. A lot of time together we spent.

He was a cute little monkey and he was very smart. He knew many tricks, things I've taught him. That little monkey will always have a place in my heart. Yes, I'm going to miss him.

A lot of things I did he'd do. He would put on his little pants and his special monkey shoes. He would get on his knees and bow his head like I do when I pray. Of course, he couldn't talk so he couldn't say what I'd say.

If he were here today I'd tell him I have learned a trick from him, too. I learned to be like Christ Jesus by way of 'monkey see, monkey do.'

Keep It Together

I've been a good boy for a long time; above commonality. In my eyes I was nothing like man; beyond his reach and understanding. I knew I was not God, for He is beyond me. No I wasn't an angel nor was I a demon. I was high but rooted. I knew my place. The world was mine but not mine. I shared it with Him.

I had my place in it – this world – but I was not of this world. I did not belong to the world. No, the world belonged to me. A piece of it anyway. Yes, it was mine. A share. I was a shareholder of the world. I owned a share of the world.

It's gone now. My share is gone, stolen away from me. Given by my hand to others. I gave what I had to those less fortunate. They gave me nothing in return.

Or did they?

They gave me what they had and I received it gleefully, not knowing that which I received would ultimately break me.

Can I blame them? No. They did nothing to me. I did it. I did it all. I gave something to hold on to and they gave something to get rid of. I kept it. I kept it.

I was naïve, then. I threw away a lot of good I received for me. I guess I just kept giving away all the good without first, acknowledging its worth, and second, taking a bit for myself. But I kept the bad.

It was burdensome. The weight brought me crashing down to the earth. That's when I was robbed. All of my shares stolen. I was kicked and beaten. I was made fun of.

Bruised, battered, and broken I stood proudly only to be ridiculed, but they couldn't take my dignity. I gave that away when I found out that it was worth nothing in this world.

Someone else needed it anyway.

I had nothing, not even a friend. When you're at the bottom no one's your friend because like you their trying to get up again. Like you they have become miserable and want you to be that way. Like you they have become vile in every manner. Like you they're weak.

We were kin. I became a nothing, a nobody; a face without a name, destined for so much, but trapped in my own naivety. Binding myself to this world in the manner of my new family.

We were all addicted to something – drugs, alcohol, sex, cigarettes, gambling, possessions, talking without listening, listening without talking, gossiping, violence, self, our own wisdom and understanding. This was home for me. This was my family. Darkness and death were our parents. Greed and want were our children. Need and desire were our masters and mistresses.

I became comfortable. Just living it up in the filth of the world.

I saw some reach up their hands and a light captured them and lifted them up. I knew what was up there but I couldn't go back. I was afraid. I was there before and I lost my place. If I go back and I lose it all again... I couldn't do it a second time. I couldn't go through the humiliation again.

There was one that I knew who's burden was bigger than mine and all her own. We would talk for long hours, sharing our loads, resting together and just being there to share a smile or a kind word. I was taken with her. But I couldn't become a burden to her. She already had a heavy load. Plus, I had a burden myself. I didn't want to add to it. Not for keeps. But we were quite fond of each other.

I remember seeing her drop her load and fall on her knees and the light captured her. Before she could reach up to be taken I yelled, "Nooo!" She saw me and reached for me asking me to come with her. I stared at her in horror and shook my head vehemently. She then grabbed hold of her burden and dragged it behind her out of the light. The light then faded.

She came straight to me and she held me, comforting me as I sat in the corner quivering with fear, and sobbing uncontrollably. She sacrificed her freedom for me. For me!

I couldn't believe it. I couldn't believe that she had done that. I couldn't believe that I actually caused her to miss out on her chance to be rid of her pain and guilt. Her burdens would have been left behind. If she had anything to carry or hold on to it would have been made lighter. And I stopped that from happening for her.

Could I have done that for her? Could I have sacrificed such a thing as that freedom? Could I? I don't think I could have at that point in time but now I think I could. But she did it then.

I knew then that she loved me. I did know what love was, but it had been so long since I had felt it outside of myself. In this place it's hard to know love. You barely see it. For me, though, I stopped seeing love outside myself long before I got grounded to earth. I barely saw love inside myself.

I, also, knew then that I have become a burden to her. She has, also, become a burden to me. A burden for each other, we became, for keeps.

The facts rushed at me, hitting me like a freight train.

Day and night – that which was considered day and night – I felt pain in my heart for this woman. I cried sometimes. I wanted to give her something more than what she gave me. Yes, she gave me a great deal but I had nothing to give her. Nothing... except... my life. I could give her... her freedom but I didn't own her freedom. I was just a burden to her. My life became a burden to her.

I tried to separate myself from her; she wouldn't leave me. I tried hurting her; bring up pain from my past, pain from her past; she still held on. I tried telling her the truth, which was I wasn't worth her; she wouldn't listen. I told her it would be beautiful to go up above the filth. She said it was beautiful just to be with me, to share our burdens, and our lives together. She said, "No matter what, I'll never leave you nor forsake you. I love you that much."

I even told her that I didn't love her and she told me it didn't matter whether I loved her or not. Shortly after she called me a liar and said, "If you didn't love me then why try to send me up to the joy that you have fallen from without you. Even when it frightens you. Not only are you afraid to go back up but you're afraid to come back down here. You're afraid to lose me – the only companion you have down here – and you speak of not loving me and not loving yourself. You love yourself so much that you pacify yourself here knowing you don't belong but telling yourself you do so that you won't suffer humiliation again.

"You're willing to be without me, sacrifice our relationship and your comfort and peace of mind for my joy. And you say you don't love me?

"Sorry but I can't go without you. I love you that much."

I cried like a baby. Never has… has anyone loved me so. Not since Him who died for me. Him who gave me my seat above others and below others. Him who granted me a share of the world. Him who I forgot for other things.

I cried. I couldn't go back with her; she wouldn't go without me. I cried. I had nothing to give her; she gave me everything. I cried. I did have something to give but I was afraid. She knew. I told her several times. She knew. She told me she was afraid, too. Not only were we afraid to go up, we were afraid to stay down.

I made up my mind then to give up and give in. She wanted to go up. She was tired of being down. She wanted me, too. She was tired of being alone.

I was tired of hiding from the truth. I wanted to go back up. I wanted her. I didn't want to be down or alone anymore. I loved her. I loved her. I love her.

Together, we knelt down. Holding hands, together, we prayed. Together, we lifted our hands. Together, we were captured by the light. Together, we were lifted up.

Our burdens were left behind…

Together.

I thank God for He loved me first. He allowed me to love Him. He continued to love me when I turned away. When I came back He still loved me. He even sent an angel to fetch me from the bottom of the barrel and set me back in my seat which He has given me from the beginning.

Lord, I praise Your holy name. Glory be to You, my God, my Rock, my Fortress, my Father who loves me eternally and unconditionally with all mercy and truth.

Thank you, my Savior, my Redeemer! You are my Hero. You rescued me, my Lord, not only from my enemy which is Yours, but from my inner-me which is the old me; buried but no completely destroyed.

I'm still fighting to keep my place and at the same time give to them less fortunate, and destroy that which is bad and of no good use. If by doing so the Lord promotes me in the ranks then so be it. Still I would be a servant. A good leader is a good follower, a good servant, giving glory to God Almighty, always.

We went up together. We're still together and we will stay together. Together we support each other, helping each other stay up. At the same time we continue to reach for them that are down and pull them up.

My experience taught me that I'm not beyond man's understanding, or beyond his reach. In actuality I didn't understand man nor did I understand God. Both man and God are near to me. I am a man. I am a son of God. I am a spirit and I am flesh. The difference between me and most men is that I strive to live in the Spirit. Not all men do that.

We all, all of mankind, start out in life at the same level that I did. My lady friend, who is now my wife, was, if not above me, on the same level as I was before we found each other at the bottom of the barrel. And everyone down there came from a higher level. Some succeeded in getting up from the bottom but others just stayed down at the bottom, unmoved and unmotivated. We've got to get it together and keep it that way.

Together.

_____

COLD TURKEY

I can remember

Way back when

I gave it all up

I quit smokin'

I said to myself

After day twenty-two

The first of the rough is over

The first step is through.

The hard part is yet to come

Get ready for step two

This is the point where

Your flesh and the devil will tempt you

That time is here now

And now I see

If I pass this test

On to step three.

Oh, the temptation!

The cravings want to take over!

Must fight the sensation!

No retreat, no surrender!

L<u>IVE</u>

I want to paint a picture

So beautiful it breaks necks,

But the only thing on my mind

Right now is sex, sex, sex, sex, sex!

I sit back, relax

Close my eyes clear my mind

Think of better days

Taking time to unwind.

I continue to stumble in the darkness

Sometimes I stumble in the light

Boy I need to let go and let God

He will make everything alright.

You say you need me

You say you want me

Is that really true?

If it is then tell me

How could this be

When you do what you do?

Make no mistake

Your life I can take

And transform it if I so desire

I can satisfy your need

Satisfy your greed

Bless with heaven, curse with hell fire

These things that you say

I know them to be true

I'm a wretched man

I admit this to you

I fear all things

To be right; to be wrong

To succeed; to fail

To be weak; to be strong

I hate mediocrity

But that's the state in which I live

I'm afraid to hold back

Afraid I don't have much to give

I created you

With all things filling you

Making you alive

I have given you

Strength and courage to

Help you survive

You have what I have

Which is a great deal

So you can always give

You must be careful

In all that you do

And watch how you live

Strive to be the best

You've got it in you

Let go of mediocrity

Don't stop half way

Complete the task

You have the ability

Face all challenges

Without fear

Live and learn

Do what's right

Day and night

It's your turn

I did what

I came to do

And that was give

I gave life

More abundantly

So abundantly live

DIVINE MULTIPLICATION

In the beginning

   There were seven days

      And on the seventh day God rested.

But one day before that day,

   Day number six

      By God's hand man was manifested.

Now God blessed man

   When he created him

      Putting everything He is into her.

They were all at once

   Both handsome and beautiful

      For one in the same they were.

Now man was made

   In the image of God

      Pay attention to this great mystery

Man was alone

   So God used his bone

      To make one into two; this is your history.

Now two becomes one

   Then becomes more

      God's mathematic computation.

Man, woman, marriage

   Children, generations

      Through God's divine multiplication.

JESUS CHRIST

Just

Eternal

Supreme

United

Stern

Caring

Head

Real

Intimate

Selfless

Triumphant

THE DREAM

I dreamed of how it would be if I were rich.

All the clothes I would have. None need a stitch.

How large my house would be; the land surrounding.

How it would be furnished. It would be astounding.

How many cars I would have, maybe five, maybe ten.

The roads I would travel from beginning to end.

The size of my yacht, and where in it I would travel.

And my private jet, oh how the secrets of the world would be unraveled.

Then I dreamed of all the friends I would have

And all of my family together enjoying a good laugh.

I dreamed this dream. It looked so good to my eyes.

I dreamed this dream, until I realized.

That this dream I dreamed was missing something.

Or someone… a perfect being.

But then He appeared as radiant and beautiful as I pictured in my mind.

He asked me a question. He asked, "For Me, would you leave this behind?"

I was at a loss for words. The dream went still.

And deep down to the bone I felt a cold chill.

I knew the answer to this question. It wasn't trivia, you know.

And I wondered, questioningly, 'Would I let it go?'

I had always said, "For him I would live."

I have said, "To Him, my life, I'd give."

But here I was, in this dream, possessing the world's best.

I looked Him in the eyes and said, finally, "Yes!"

And suddenly, with a flash of light, everything I had was gone.

Everything in sight... which left Him and I alone.

He then pointed to the right. I looked and there stood a mirror of full length.

I looked back at Him and then at my reflection seeing in me His strength.

"Go now," He said to me, "and know that I am with you always."

"Go now," He said, "for you have received no end to your days."

"Spread My glory throughout the land. Tell the people who I am.

Tell them of the gift you received. Tell them to join and follow Me.

This is the Cross that you must bear.

Tell them about our Father and how much He care.

Find the lost Sheep and bring them home.

Let them know that in the fold they're never alone.

I love you," He said. Then He turned to leave.

When He was gone I awoke and found myself on my knees.

My Enemy

I've walked behind many

Treading carefully

Watching where I stepped

Trying to follow righteously

I've walked quietly

Amongst many who spoke freely

Keeping close guard on my tongue

For I feared my enemy

In that time

I've learned

In that time

I've discerned

My biggest enemy

Is very close to me

And once I subdue him

I'd be free.

My biggest

Enemy

Is the

Old me

He hangs around

Continuously

Trying to seduce me with

Old memories

How is it that

He lingers near

Though I'm born again?

Because we

Were partners there

We were friends back then.

But now we're enemies and he's trying to get back in

He knows I don't hate him but he's got to submit

To the New Man within, to the Spirit that abides in me.

Yes he must go legit.

Until then we'll be close

But we won't be tight

I will walk with Christ and sacrifice

My flesh daily; yes to the end I'll fight.

GOD IS THE REASON (WHY I LOVE YOU)

For some reason

I love you.

For some reason

I do.

Is it your honesty

Or how you complete me?

Is it your beauty

Or dependability?

Is it what you do to me

Or is it the words you speak?

Is it what you bring out of me

Or my secrets that you keep?

Is it your strength of character

Or your spiritual presence in a room?

There's gotta be a reason

For we did jump the broom.

Is it your humility

And the way you call me "lord"?

Is it your company

On this ship we're aboard?

Sailing toward the same goal;

The dream within our hearts.

Eternally devoted to one another;

Not even death can keep us apart.

But the *reason* I love you,

And I know it's true,

Is God in me,

And God in you.

For through Him

We were created,

Joined together,

And dedicated

To Him,

And to one another.

Understanding fully

What it means to be lovers.

And that's why I love you,

As you can see,

The reason is

God in you and God in me.

You Are Not Alone (Divine Multiplication II)

When I was young and alone

I was full of insecurity

But now that I'm grown

I see that one can equal three

God, Jesus, and the Holy Ghost

Make up the Divine Trinity

One in the same

Yet three separate entities

I added myself

And the number changed to four

But when multiplied

The number was as before

Then I got married

And you know in married life

Two become one

Though husband and wife

But when you put God at the head

It's plain to see

That three separate entities

Becomes one trinity

But God is a Trinity

Him, Jesus Christ and the Spirit

Which is Holy

And five is a "Quintity"

But through all this counting

What do you see?

Do you see how silly

Man can be?

God said, "I Am That I Am."

Which means to me

That He is all things

Everything I need

But men in Moses' time

Couldn't understand that concept

So God was patient

His promises kept.

His mathematics

Still holding true

Trickling though generations

To reach me and you

So whether young or old

I hope I helped you see

God made and can be in all things

Even you and me

But beware, I don't want to scare

Any below or above

Though your will may be strong do no wrong;

Do all things in love

If you're without love

You're without God

Who is all the things we need

When times get hard

I wrote all this to say

One thing to thee

You are not alone

God is with you as He is with me.

GUARDIAN ANGELS

Some don't believe

They choose not to

For to believe

Like I do

Will make us all

Susceptible

We'll have to accept God

And His word as true

Guardian Angels

Angels of God

They are all about us

They work really hard

Their mission: Protect us

From those wicked things

In us and around us

What joy and peace that brings

Here in Iraq

Skeptics wouldn't believe

But true blessings from God

My unit and I received

We've made some mistakes, been attacked

But were made to survive

It's by His grace

That we're still alive

"Heroes" and "Warriors"

Some might want to call us

But God answers prayers

Ours and yours for us

A hedge around us

These angels are

Fighting tooth and nail

To keep us from harm

They are what you wanted

They are what we asked for

They protected us well

What more could we ask for

They fight and don't flee

They've rescued us

When we were afraid

They comforted us	Fall on our knees
	And begin to pray
When we became angry	Even if we don't know
Because we were still there	What to say
They calmed our spirits	Just call on the Lord
And filled us with cheer	And He will hear
These angels of God	He'll send His angels
They trained us too	To combat your fears
So in any situation	
We know what to do	That's what happened Over There.

DEVINE SUBTRACTION

I know you heard

Devine Multiplication

But get ready for

A new sensation

This is a message

Full of spiritual nutrition

It's only purpose

Help your spiritual condition

I hope you understand

And get satisfaction

From this message

Devine Subtraction

People are always looking

Always looking to

Add something to their lives

Leaving no room

For what they need

What they want overwhelms them

"Let it go. Follow me."

That's what He tells them

But do they listen

No, they just hold on

Thinking that which doesn't kill me

Only makes me strong

But their weakened by the things

That don't belong

I know it's true

'Cause I used to sing the same song

I opened up, let Him in

So He can fill me

He took some things, threw it out

I thought it'll kill me

I shook and shivered in a corner

Feeling badly

He touched my head and said

"I love you madly."

This is the message of

Divine Subtraction

I hope you understand

And get satisfaction

This is a lesson so

Learn while you listen

It is the only way to

Heavenly Addition

This is the message of

Devine Subtraction

Let Him remove

All of those distractions

In your life

Causing you to be a fraction

Trust in God

Should be your only action

Let Him take it away

And He'll add to you

All things that are good

Yes good for you

Things lovely, things holy

Things that are true

He'll throw away your mess

And make you brand new

He'll pick you up

And when He set you down

He'll place your feet

On the solid ground

If you look you'll notice

You've been turned around

Filled with the Spirit of power

And love and a mind that's sound

You'll get a new heart

Filled with grace

He'll hand you a baton and say

"Run this race."

Run fast run slow

Pick your pace

Finish the run

No matter where you place

I used to run slow

Couldn't run fast

Looked back and saw I was

Burdened by my past

He cut the rope

Burden gone

Ocean floor

Dead and gone

This is the message of

Divine Subtraction

I hope you understand
And get satisfaction
This is a lesson so
Learn while you listen
It is the only way to
Heavenly Addition

This is the message of
Divine Subtraction
God is watching you
Recording every action
He doesn't like you
On the side of opposition
He's urging you
To make a decision

I run this race for Him
He set me free
His yoke is easy, burden light
It doesn't hinder me
God is good all the time
Taste and see
And all the time God is good
Do you hear me?

Bad subtracted; good added
That's His arithmetic
Multiply your faith
To help you stick
To the path straight and narrow
Saints on the side
They cheer you on
Haters try to break your stride
Put Him first. Eyes on Him
And you will fly
On eagles' wings. Pay attention
I'mma tell you why

This is the message of
Devine Subtraction
New life in Christ
That's satisfaction
New day, new year
You're still living
Praise to God with all your might
You should be giving
Choose life choose Christ
That's my suggestion

Don't let the devil

Cloud your perception

Follow Him while you live

Twenty-four seven

Eventually you'll be with Him

Up in heaven

This the message of

Divine subtraction

I hope you understand

And get satisfaction

This is a lesson

So learn while you listen

It is the only way

To heavenly addition.

True Love

If a woman wants to be treated like a queen, she must first take off her princess crown. She can only be daddy's little princess for so long. She must take off her princess crown and receive the crown from her new king.

Be ye careful though princesses. Every man with a crown is not a king. There are those who pose to get you to take off your clothes and curl your toes just to leave you with tears streaming down cheeks and nose. That blows. True kings don't rock crowns in crowds.

Ladies if you got a man and you think he's a king just because he gives you everything, do a check. Is he the head upon you, the neck, and allow you to turn him when it makes sense? Or does he just ignore you and order you around like he's your superior and not your equal?

Yes, Adam was first, but he was sad and lonely and needed a lift. God lulled him to sleep, removed a rib and brought him a gift. A woman, bright and beautiful, to him, Adam, she was comparable. God called her his help meet. Not his mate, nor his mat, no sort of place for his feet. She was to help him in all his tasks; he was to keep her for he asked, "LORD, what about me? They all have someone, the beast of the field, the foul of the air, the creepy crawly things and the fish of the sea, but what about me, LORD? What about me?" God answered his prayer, and sent him Eve. He didn't give him what he didn't need. God kept it real. He knew what to do. He gave him a woman. Someone he compared to.

Men get your head on straight, pose your weight, be the man you're supposed to be. Ladies get it right, keep it tight, and help that man to see. He's a king, a descendent of kings, sacrificing all things for his queen, who's fathered by a king, who respects him in everything.

True love is a sacrifice. True love is respect. True love is an action, not just words said.

The Boy

Let he who has an ear hear. Let he who has an eye see.

He was born, dreamed, grew up, dreamed again, grew some more, dreamed elaborately, became grown, chased the dream, and grew older still chasing.

The dream is too big, he said to himself. How do I achieve it? No answer came. He figured, 'I'll chop it up into small goals.' So he did just that. But even they were too big.

'I'll make them even smaller more achievable goals,' he said. And he did but then he saw that there were many. He didn't know where to start. He decided to organize them from the easiest to the hardest. Now he was set. The puzzle was put together and he was on his way.

One day a storm blew in. This storm was powerful. It would bring trouble to any and all who got in its way. He just happened to be in the way of the storm. The storm hit him and hit him hard and scattered all the pieces to his puzzle. When he went back to put the puzzle together again he found that pieces were missing, leaving holes in it - some large some small. He searched for the pieces and could not find them.

He found some other pieces but they did not fit. He decided to go with what he got and see where it would take him. He found himself in many places. Some places took him far away from his dream but he held on to the big picture. Some places introduced him to people who decided to help. Though they meant well they were a hindrance to him and he had to leave them behind. Some places introduced him to people who had dreams as broken as his and they decided to join their dreams to his to make it a better picture. Though they were encouraging he found that their dreams brought more drama than anything and he had to let them go.

The boy, who is now a man in his years, did not learn through his previous experiences very valuable lessons. Because of this, the boy, though full grown, is still a boy. His puzzle still missed pieces. His dream still not realized.

There are two things the boy could do to become a man; 1) Take his time and learn the lessons that were missed that will bring the missing pieces back to him so that the puzzle can be complete, re-enforced, and framed causing the big picture to be made whole and achievable. 2) Let go of the boyhood dream and re-establish himself as a man with a dream that can be attached to anyone's dream and be achievable through their efforts as well as his own. The lost dream would never be achieved but the dreams of others will. This he learned from a very wise man.

He didn't know what to do. He wanted to achieve his dream. He wanted others to achieve theirs too. He stood still as fear began to take hold of him. He could not move. This was unbelievable to him. Let go of his dream? Help others achieve theirs? What kind of choice is that? Take time and learn the missed lessons? Go through another terrible storm? Meet the same old people that meant him no harm but lent him no help?

He asked the wise man, "How do I achieve either of these? How do I choose? Either way I'm letting go of something. What would you choose?"

The wise man said, "I have already made my choice. I cannot make yours for you. I can tell you that the choice I made was best for me. You must choose what's best for you."

The boy/man stood there. He stood there staring in astonishment. Suddenly resolve came over him as he made a decision that was not one of the choices. He stood there and decided not to choose either. For neither were appealing to him. And so he stood. Neither did he move forward, nor did he move back. He turned neither left nor right. He simply stood. None could move him. None could encourage him. He just stood as life past him by, and his dream faded away.

Queen In Her Own Right

Hard as nails. Tough as a bull dog. Not easy to get along with if you wanna play leap frog.

Never held by fear. Don't live with regret. Show love and respect or she'll put you in check.

Lips soft and tender. Eyes sharp and penetrating. She's never demanding but don't keep her waiting.

Heart exposed. If you want it you can take it. Be warned. Don't ever break it.

Cause she's a queen in her own right. Aware of her own might. But don't need a man that she must fight. She likes being cared for don't need to be kept. She keeps herself. Understand that or step.

Cheat on her... wrong. Lie to her... wrong. Lie on her... homey I hope that you're strong.

Cause the force that she comes with is nothing but truth. Dig a ditch with your lies she'll help bury you.

Loves her girl and her boy. Gives them gifts full of joy. She has sweetness in heart. No need for Chips A'Hoy.

Come at her the wrong way, the first time she's kind. Do it again and you'll lose your mind.

Cause she's a queen in her own right. Aware of her own might. But don't need a man that she must fight. She likes being cared for don't need to be kept. She keeps herself. Understand that or step.

Now a woman like this is one in a million. Men try to play but instead catch feelings.

Look into her eyes and you'll lose control. You'll try to hold back but you'll bear your soul.

You'll wanna give it to her, everything you are. Even as a friend you'll want every part.

Her body, her mind, her heart, her time, her sunshine, her rain, her joy, her pain.

She may let you add to her. She may let you take away. But if she let you don't ever go astray. 'Cause she'll let you keep going till you're so far away that you won't find your way back on any day.

Cause she's a queen in her own right. Aware of her own might. But don't need a man that she must fight. She likes being cared for don't need to be kept. She keeps herself. Understand that or step.

Real Work, True Worth

"If it were easy, it wouldn't be worth it." "Anything worth having at all is worth waiting and working for."

Trust this though, the work doesn't stop or get easier once you've gotten it. You have to put in more time and go the extra mile to hold on to it. You can't just be all you can be. NO! You have to be more than that. You have to continue to improve, otherwise, you will lose everything that you ever wanted, needed, and loved. So keep pressing on because the journey is not over. The work is not done because you got what you wanted, needed, or loved. No, the work just got a little more complicated. Look to the "Divine Manager" of our life's work for guidance on how to manage your workload the way He manages His. Now go to work and do the work. Don't just put in work. Become a master of it.

HEART/MIND

Oh my my my. Look at me now. Absence makes the heart grow fonder. Absence makes the heart ponder.

What is it that the heart wants? What is it that the heart needs? Where does it belong? How does its weakness make it strong?

A throng of passion burns within. Its hearth ablaze; righteousness or sin? It knows not, but the mind deciphers. The heart is blind. 'Tis why faith's its comforts. It passes through a den of vipers, but not ever slowed by their efforts.

The heart moves, it doesn't know why, the soul of a man to an all out cry. The mind understands but it doesn't share. For if it does that means it cares.

Put them together and u will see it's true; the rollercoaster ride is beautiful.

To Thine Own Self Be True

To thine own self be true?

Was that directed at me, or was it for you?

To thine own self be true.

Easier said than done. I try will you?

To thine own self be true.

Ask me and I'll say, but I have words for you.

To thine own self be true.

But look deeper than self. See your heart. Is it you?

I tossed and turned

These words in the air; tucked them deep in the ground.

I dragged them along

Filled with despair; footfalls matching heart's pound.

I ran from them

Afraid of what I'd see if I turned 'round.

Fatigued, I stopped

Let them catch me, and this is what I found.

A reflection of me

Only not me; there was no fearful frown.

Oh my, oh me

How could this be? My frown upside down.

My heart beat is racing

Mind spinning and chasing thoughts of myth and logic.

My reflection smiling

Flexing, profiling without anything toxic.

To thine own self be true?

You dare me; I dare you.

Look at your heart

Is it like mine; open and beautiful?

Seeing what I saw

Knowing what I knew; I trip I fall.

But angels caught me up

Held me true; for Jesus paid it all.

Past, present, future

Lost, broken, found; mirror shattered one whole.

To thine own self be true

Might I be so bold? Yes, for God's plan has saved my soul.

Hidden Away

Hidden away
Is the man of good standing.
The man who puts forth a good work.

Hidden away
Is the man of understanding.
The man who studies to show himself approved.

Hidden away
Is the man of courage.
The man who boldly stands, and fearlessly delivers the Word of God.

Hidden away
Is the man, the proud man.
The man who is proud of himself but not because of himself. The man who is proud of God who has made him who he is.

Hidden away
Is that man of pride.
That man's pride is in the fact that God knows him and he knows God.

Hidden away
Is that man of love.
That man who loves God more than anything.

Hidden away
Is that man who loves.
That man who loves others because his Father taught him how to love.

Hidden away
Is that man of praise; that man of worship.
That man of prayer and subjugation.

Hidden away
Is that man who stands in the gap.
That man who prays for his enemies as well as his friends and families.

Hidden away
Is the man of peace.
That man who tries to calm the seas and quiet the storms.
That man who wants to believe in others even when his gut tells him he's wrong.

Why is that man hiding?
You might ask.
What does he fear?

But you don't understand.
That man is not hiding
Of his own free will.

That man is bound and gagged.
Hidden away in the darkest corner of his temple.
He's blindfolded so he cannot see.

His hands and feet are bound so that he does not fight or flee.
His mouth is gagged so that he cannot speak out against his enemy.
But he's able to smell the putrid and ransid odor of his temple; unkempt and unclean.

He can hear the foul language used to describe him.
Words of belittlement. Words humiliating.
Words of disgust; bordering on rage.

He wants to squirm forward or slide away from the abuse.
But he's caged in this corner. Shackled about the waist and chained to the wall.

He feels his binds irritating his skin and cannot scratch.

He feels the continuous poking and prodding of the enemy along with the occasional beating and torture.
He wants to cry out or lash out but he refuses to give his enemy the satisfaction of hate returned.

You see, he loves his enemy as he loves himself. He does for his enemy that which he would do for himself if he could.

He moans his discomfort but not as a complaint.
No, he moans in prayer for his enemy's body, heart, and soul.
He moans in praise and thanksgiving to the Lord.
He moans in worship to the same.

He stands on every Word of God though he cannot see them to read them and cannot speak them clearly, but he knows them for they are written on his heart.

He understands his position for he understands his enemy's desire to break his will and ultimately make him change his mind about the God in which he believes. However, he could not be shaken. He could not be moved, for he was approved through his studies and knowledge of God.

His courage was unwavering for he had a peace that surpassed all understanding, a joy unspeakable, a love unconditional, a strength that was his by way of Him who was far greater. A pride that was in himself but not of himself. A pride in and of God. He had a belief that said, "All things work together for the good of them that love the Lord."

He didn't ask "when" or "why"? he simply stayed focused on his mission and on Him who called him forth.

As time goes on he can feel the pain in his enemy's broken heart. He can feel his enemy's loneliness. He can feel his enemy's sadness. Every condition of his enemy he can feel, but this only causes him to love his enemy so much more.

More and more his enemy is breaking down.
More and more his enemy is revealing himself.
More and more his enemy is becoming his friend.
More and more his enemy is visiting without abusing.

He is still bound but loosely.
Still he is gagged but loosely.
Still he is blindfolded but loosely.
Still he is uncomfortable but less irritated
Still his temple is a mess but it smells better.
Still he hears his enemy's words.
But less disgust and humiliation is hurled at him.

Still he prays though he's hidden away.
His desire; to be released one day.
To finish the work he has started.
To become one with his enemy.
Before they're both dearly
Departed and never
Realize the dream
That God has
Placed in
His heart.

I can't wait for that day
When I'm no longer
Hidden away
Hiding
Myself.

ROOTED

Rooted and growing. Covered and showing. Standing and glowing in the glory of God.

Two separate souls become one whole. Supported by the pole, sometimes it seems hard.

For two to become one and never be undone in this long run. Even when we're apart.

That's why in happiness our marriage is blessed. Though there's some stress, we'll stay one heart.

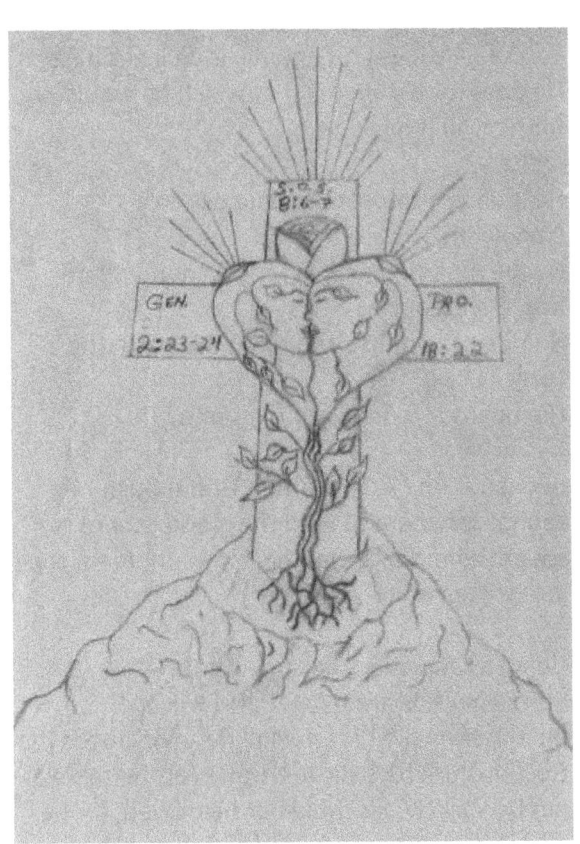

THE CLOSE

I hope what I've written doesn't douse you with anger.

My hope is that it aroused you to meet the stranger.

An alien, foreign to us all.

I encourage you to meet him. Simply, get a glimpse.

Let him feed the mustard seed. Your tree will never go limp.

He knew us before the fall.

Of this world we never were. Of him we are.

In his teachings he left behind he says he's never too far.

So get to know him. Better yet let him know you.

From this world he brought us forth. To this earth we go forth.

Our flesh alone; our spirits go home.

It's not about what you do.

Basically, I hope and pray these words fed a hunger inside you; appeased your desires through and through. Rebuilt what was broken. Closed what was open. Opened what was closed, and broke through what was built. Just to "touch" you in the way you needed to be "touched".

ACKNOWLEDGEMENTS

I'd like to thank my mom and dad for recognizing my talent and encouraging me to grow in it. Mom, you don't know how your words forced me to look deeper within to find the truth of what needed to be said instead of saying what I figured others would want to hear.

I thank my sisters and brothers. My sisters, for always sneaking, and reading my stuff when I didn't want you to, and then laughing at me to my face. Though a lot of times I was embarrassed, those moments helped me to recognize that sometimes there's comedy in a story. No matter how serious it seems. My brothers, I appreciate the encouragement; the push to be creative. I especially appreciate how you both had outdone me in areas that I thought I was the expert (art, music, dance, and sports). Being outdone helped me to focus on the area I am actually pretty good at.

To my cousins, aunts and uncles, thank you for always encouraging me in all things I set my hands to.

To my wife; thanks for being an inspiration in my life.

To my children, thanks for just being there and giving me things to write about through life lessons.

To my friends, old and new, tried and true, thanks for just being there.

Some of you have read, or heard poems from this book when they were birthed. Thanks for encouraging me to keep going after the dream.

Most of all I would like to thank God for blessing me with this one of many talents. It is through him that I am able to do anything. It is through him that I am awarded the time to do anything. And I thank him for the will, the drive, and the courage to complete and publish this work.

HAUNTED BY YOUR BEAUTY

He dreamed of her.

Who was she?

He didn't know.

It didn't matter.

Not to him.

He wanted her so.

He gave chase.

As she flitted

In and out of view.

Naked as a jay bird,

Shadowed by trees,

Lighted by the moon.

She seemed to enjoy it

This was her game

He enjoyed it, too.

Never has he felt so alive

Stimulated

Wonderful!

He started to gain on her

Able to see in detail

Her body from the rear.

Excited he ran harder

Reaching for her

He was so near.

Oh no! Something happened!

Then he realized

He'd tripped and fell

She turned round, running backwards

Shrugged her shoulders

And mouthed, "Oh well."

She turned and continued

He pounded the ground

And got back to his feet

He had seen her full frontal

He continued to chase

He'd seen her beauty complete.

   He ran and ran

The moon became covered by clouds

Still he ran, he ran in vain.

   He became tired and distracted

He needed rest.

He would not catch up with her again.

   At least not this night

But he was still hopeful

As he began to shiver and shake.

   It was dark

He was cold and alone

   Suddenly he came awake.

   He sat up in his bed

Wiped the sweat from his head

And slid beneath the covers

   He thought, "I will catch you one day,

Believe what I say,

And then we will be lovers."

   He lay on his back

Closed his eyes and relaxed

And took a breath that was real deep.

   Then he turned on his side

Comforted inside

And was fast asleep.

www.ingramcontent.com/pod-product-compliance
Lightning Source LLC
Chambersburg PA
CBHW081023040426
42444CB00014B/3330